DATE DUE

HIGHSMITH 45-112

SPOTLIGHT ON
THE
EDWARDIAN
ERA

Christopher Martin

Wayland

SPOTLIGHT ON HISTORY

Spotlight on the Age of Enlightenment
Spotlight on the Age of Exploration and Discovery
Spotlight on the Age of Revolution
Spotlight on the Age of Scientific Discovery
Spotlight on the Agricultural Revolution
Spotlight on the Cold War
Spotlight on the Collapse of Empires
Spotlight on the Edwardian Era
Spotlight on Elizabethan England
Spotlight on the English Civil War
Spotlight on the First World War
Spotlight on the Industrial Revolution
Spotlight on Industry in the Twentieth Century
Spotlight on the Interwar Years
Spotlight on Medieval Europe
Spotlight on the Napoleonic Wars
Spotlight on Nineteenth-Century Imperialism
Spotlight on Post-War Europe
Spotlight on the Raj
Spotlight on the Reformation
Spotlight on Renaissance Europe
Spotlight on the Rise of Modern China
Spotlight on the Russian Revolution
Spotlight on the Second World War
Spotlight on the Stuarts
Spotlight on the Victorians

Cover illustration: A Ball at the Savoy Hotel, The Illustrated London News 1911
Editor: Rhoda Nottridge
Consultant: Dr A. Howkins, School of Cultural and Community Studies, University of Sussex

First published in 1987 by Wayland (Publishers) Ltd
61 Western Road, Hove, East Sussex BN3 1JD, England

British Library Cataloguing in Publication Data
Martin, Christopher, *1939–*
Spotlight on the Edwardian era.—(Spotlight on history)
1. Great Britain—Social life and customs—20th century—Juvenile literature
I. Title
941.082'3   DA566.4
ISBN 1-85210-008-7
Typeset, printed and bound in the UK at The Bath Press, Avon

CONTENTS

1 A WORLD IN TRANSITION

On the 22 January 1901 Queen Victoria died, after the longest reign in English history. It seemed a great turning point. The *Yorkshire Post* correspondent watched the coffin carried from the Isle of Wight, where the Queen had died at her Osborne home: 'Ten miles of warships line the Solent . . . and slowly, silently passed between [them] the royal yacht. The coffin on her deck was in full view of all, covered with a pall of white satin with the Royal Standard thrown across it. Boom! Boom! go the guns . . . The sun is setting in a mass of flame and its last shafts flash red upon the sparkling crown that lies upon the coffin . . .'

One of the ten mile line of Royal Navy warships which honoured Queen Victoria as her body was taken by yacht from the Isle of Wight where she died.

King Edward VII, whose coronation procession is seen here, seemed to usher in a 'golden era' after the long years of Victorian gloom.

The new King, Edward VII, extrovert and pleasure-loving, presented a brighter face of monarchy after the long, late-Victorian gloom. The King, also an Emperor presiding over the vast British Empire, gave his name to the era up to 1910, when he died, and beyond, as the mood of his reign still coloured British life up to the outbreak of war in August 1914.

The accession of the new King coincided with the keenly-awaited beginning of the twentieth century. Technology, much of it from the USA, symbolized the sense of change and progress. To most Edwardians, these inventions were like new toys. They could not anticipate just how much electricity, the motor car, the aeroplane, Marconi's wireless signals or moving pictures were to transform human life.

Electricity was one of the technical wonders of the era. This cartoon expressed concern about the safety of the new network of electric wires.

Less obvious were the changes in the social order in all advanced countries: in the status of women, in the rising power of the working class, in the growth of urban life with its new interests and entertainment and in the increasing influence of the state on the lives of everyone.

Over the Edwardian era hung the threat of European war. This was the last age of empires. Those splendidly-uniformed crowned heads of Europe, glimpsed in the primitive newsreels of Queen Victoria's funeral, became leaders of hostile, heavily-armed alliances that split the continent. The Great War they fought produced an altered world order and hastened the rise of power of the USA.

After 1918, the wealthy looked back to the Edwardian era and saw a lost golden age. Today we can see a harsher picture of a restless world in transition.

King Edward and Queen Alexandra were the centre of society, the élite among rich British families.

2 SOCIAL CONTRASTS: RICH AND POOR

Edwardian Britain was characterized by acute inequalities of wealth. The vast accumulation of riches created in the late nineteenth century was enjoyed by a tiny minority of the population. Leo Chiozza Money described, in *Riches and Poverty*, how the United Kingdom was made up of 'a great multitude of poor people, veneered with a thin layer of the comfortable and rich.' He found that 1.25 million people took a third of the national income, only 5 million half of it, and 38 million shared the rest.

The lives of the wealthy

The rich and powerful formed 'Society', an élite described by a modern historian as 'a pyramid of interlocking spiders' webs'. At the centre of the web was the King himself. Nineteenth-century society had been based on great landowning families: in 1873, only 4,000 people possessed half the land of England and Wales. The 'new rich', whose

Lunch in the open air at Falconhurst, one of the great Edwardian country houses.

A society party during the London Season of 1903. Edwardian social critics protested at the expenditure on clothes, food and decorations.

money was made from industry or commerce, had begun to penetrate society. In his mother's reign, Edward had admitted people such as Sir Thomas Lipton, the grocer, or Sir Blundell Maple, the store owner, to his social set, valuing their financial advice. When Edward took the throne, money seemed to become the chief standard of social worth. As land values fell in the agricultural slump after 1875, the old aristocracy began to become city businessmen themselves. An elderly Victorian aristocrat noted that 'there are now many scions of noble houses who exhibit as much shrewdness in driving bargains in the City as a South African millionaire himself'.

Upper-class life revolved around the 'Season', when, from May to August, the rich came to London to participate in a series of social events. Balls, receptions (perhaps even at Buckingham Palace itself), the theatre, Royal Ascot, the Eton-Harrow cricket match were all dedicated to maintaining or advancing family status. That measure of acceptance within society, the network of afternoon calls – when splendid, crested carriages or motor cars carried the rich to each other's town houses – was, according to an etiquette manual, 'the basis on which that great structure, society, rests'. The magnificence of Edwardian high life was best seen at the dinner table. Edwardians, like their King, had huge appetites: ten to fourteen courses were commonplace. 'No age since Nero,' commented the diplomat, Harold Nicholson, 'can show such unlimited addiction to food'. Table displays were dramatic: one guest at a party for twenty-four, counted 362 dishes and plates in use. After dinner, the guests could stroll on the red carpet and striped awning which were put out in front of the house where a ball was taking place. For the young, the Season was a marriage market. Young ladies 'came out' at eighteen when they were presented to the King as 'debutantes'. In their elaborate gowns, 'a mass of silver, opalescent gold or moonlight sequins', protected by their chaperones, they filled in the tiny dance programmes, which gave them a succession of partners. Eligible young men were showered with invitations.

The emptiness of the social round of the Season irritated some young Edwardians. The poet Julian Grenfell disliked his mother's parties: 'bows and grimaces and hurry and clatter and insincerity, women twittering like tired birds and men tinkling like empty glasses'. Charles Masterman, in *The Condition of England*, saw the Season as 'talk, talk, talk . . . what does it all mean? No one knows . . . It presents the appearance of a complicated machine which has escaped the control of all human volition'. The rich seemed 'a company of tired children, flushed and uncomfortable from the too violent pursuit of pleasure'.

In Edwardian times, the display of the Season was complicated by 'conspicuous consumption', a recently-invented American phrase. What the American novelist Upton Sinclair called 'the crude scattering of wealth' by the industrial rich of Newport and New York set the fashion. As examples of the 'mad race for display', Sinclair had seen a woman whose teeth were filled with diamonds, and another who boasted of never appearing twice in the same dress. The luxurious shops of London's Bond Street supplied similar anecdotes: a skirt made of one piece of eleventh-century lace, the shoes cut from medieval velvet. The rich also loved vast building projects. Some of their new country homes, like Andrew Carnegie's Skibo Castle in Scotland, were more splendid than the King's palaces. One man moved a considerable hill to open up the view from his house; another built a billiard room underwater in his lake. '"Waste" is written large over a very substantial proportion of the national expenditure', commented Masterman. 'Where one house sufficed, now two are demanded, where a dinner of a certain quality,

Expensive and elaborate hats were an important part of the society lady's complicated wardrobe.

The 'slimy pavements and screaming streets' of city slums, described by Edwardian social investigators.

now a dinner of a superior quality, where clothes or dresses or flowers, now more clothes, more dresses, more flowers.'

The lives of the poor

Pioneer sociologists went among the 'slimy pavements and the screaming streets' of poor city districts to study them systematically, bringing to light the appalling poverty which had gone unnoticed, or at least unacknowledged, for years. Lady Florence Bell, the wife of a wealthy Middlesborough ironmaster, described life in her home town in *At the Works* (1907). Here was the industrial mushroom town, clustered round the iron foundry: 'the grey streets ... all set in a background of greyness, in a devastated landscape under a grey sky'. The 'struggling, striving' worker could have a fair but precarious standard of living, but the dangerous path beside the moulds where molten metal ran was 'an emblem of the road of life along which he must walk'. The women's life was harsher: poverty and pollution caused heavy infant mortality. (650 of the 2,072 Middlesborough deaths of 1904 were children under one year.) Women dragged their skirts in the mud to avoid revealing their dreadful footwear, the 'boiled boots' taken from rubbish dumps and resold on street markets.

16

Charles Booth, a rich shipping merchant, described London's East End in his massive study, *The Life and Labour of the People of London*. Teams of interviewers surveyed various districts, calling at every house. Booth sadly concluded that 30 per cent of London's population was living in poverty. He described the poor as 'brought up in stifling rooms, with scanty food, in the midst of births and deaths. Their life is the life of savages.'

To Edwardians, the work of Seebohm Rowntree seemed the more shocking because it concerned the apparently pleasant cathedral city of York. In *Poverty, A Study of Town Life*, he defined a poverty line, based on a minimum income for rent and food: 5 per cent of wage-earners lived below the line, and 28 per cent near it. He portrays the miserable dwellings in back streets: 'House No 4: two rooms, seven inmates . . . smell of room from dirt and bad air unbearable . . . children pale, starved-looking and only half-clothed, one boy with hip disease and other with sores over face . . .' Rowntree's revelation that half the

A London family living in one room in 1903. Overcrowding, dirt and poor diet were features of lower-class life in the cities.

potential Army recruits from York, between 1897–1901, were rejected as unfit caused particular concern. Was the health of the Empire in decay? The Conservative government's Committee on Physical Deterioration (1903–4) was an immediate result.

The American writer Jack London followed a trend set by Victorian social investigators by disguising himself as a down-and-out and sharing the life of the poor in London's East End. In *People of the Abyss*, he described the homeless sleeping rough, 'a welter of rags and filth, of all manner of loathsome skin diseases, open sores, bruises, grossness. . . . A chill, raw wind was blowing and these creatures huddled there in their rags.' He was astonished to see the depths of poor men's hunger: 'From the slimy, spittle-drenched sidewalk, they were picking up bits of orange peel, apple skins and grape stems, and they were eating them.

It is hard to believe the vast wealth of the British Empire, when confronted with pictures of the poverty in London in the 1900s.

A 'sweated labour' workshop in London's East End in 1904. A woman dies of tuberculosis in an overcrowded room.

And this was in the heart of the greatest, wealthiest and most powerful Empire the world has ever seen'. The only thing that was beautiful in this 'city of degradation' was the sight of children dancing to the street barrel organ.

Government Reports were also a voice of the public conscience. 'Sweated labour' in the East End caused dismay: here a girl could receive three pence for sewing twenty-four shirts. An Inspector described a workshop: 'There was a large bed on which the mother of the family was dying of consumption. Although it was summer, there was a large fire in the room, before which the husband was at his work as a tailor, pressing cloth and so filling the air with steam.'

A grim Christmas dinner at a Marylebone workhouse. Critics protested at this herding together of the poor and unfortunate.

In 1902, 1½ million people were still affected by the Poor Law. In a Royal Commission Report, protests were made about the old workhouses where 'the worthy old man' was herded in with 'the hardened, sodden loafer'. 80,000 down-and-outs used the casual wards, some of which were worse than prisons: 'The cells are dark and cold; the bare stone floor, with one rug, is the only sleeping place. During the day, the men are locked in solitary pens and kept for nine hours at stone breaking, the hardest and most monotonous toil that has yet been devised.'

It was such revelations about the poor, what Masterman called 'the twisted, distorted life, which lives and grows and dies in the darkness', that helped to stimulate Edwardian social reform.

3 TOWN AND COUNTRY

By 1901, Britain had become an urban nation. Of 41.5 million people counted by the census, only a quarter still lived in the country. London was the most remarkable 'conurbation' (a new Edwardian word) with its population of 6.5 million. 'Suburbia' was spreading round it, and other large cities, as better transport allowed commuters to live further out. Most of this suburban sprawl was un-planned and erected by small builders. In 1904, a *Times* correspondent protested: 'The speculative builder descends upon green fields . . . To surround London with acres of such streets is to produce a district of appalling monotony, ugliness and dullness.'

Pioneers showed that a better environment was possible. In his *Garden Cities of Tomorrow*, Ebenezer Howard proposed new towns of 30,000 people, set in open country to allow 'fresh air, sunlight, breathing space, playing room'. An association built the first Garden

Thousands of tramps were harshly treated in what were called casual wards. Religious slogans were placed over the crude box beds.

City at Letchworth in 1903. With its attractive range of housing, it was hailed by the *Times* as 'our ideal of the small town of the future'. Its architect, Raymond Unwin, later created Hampstead Garden Suburb, planned as a balanced community of cottages and larger houses with gardens, near to the city.

Town planning also received official encouragement, perhaps after a Manchester reformer, T. C. Horsfall, described how Germany had produced better housing for its workers, thereby improving their health and working efficiency. The Liberal government's Housing and Town Planning Act of 1909 promised 'the home healthy, the town pleasant, the city dignified', but little was actually achieved before 1914.

City transport
Urban transport changed dramatically during the Edwardian years. The electric tram, first seen in northern cities, then, after 1901, in London, became the 'gondola of the people', giving ordinary city-dwellers much more mobility. Tramway mileage doubled between 1900 and 1907. However, the more flexible motor bus soon proved a formidable rival.

Ebenezer Howard's Garden City at Letchworth, seen here in 1913, was an answer to the casual suburban sprawl near large cities.

The first electric tram in London, 1901. The new service was cheap and gave ordinary people more mobility.

The handful seen in London in 1905 had become 3,000 by 1913. The reliable 'B' type bus, of the London General Omnibus Company, painted red and plastered with advertisements, became a familiar part of the capital's streets. The open tops became a forest of umbrellas in wet weather. The horse-drawn cab was dying, too. In 1904, 11,000 hansoms shared London with two 'taximeter cars'; by 1910, there were 6,000 taxis to 5,000 hansoms, which gradually disappeared. The private motor car was already complicating the city traffic problem. A 1913 Report of the Board of Trade observed: 'The convenience of the mechanically propelled vehicle for passenger purposes very rapidly asserted itself and today it accounts for fully 94 per cent of the passenger vehicles met with on the roads round London. Street accidents are an unfortunate phase of the traffic problem ...' The great twentieth century slaughter on the roads had begun.

The last days of horse transport in London at the turn of the century. By 1914, motor vehicles dominated city traffic.

The Edwardians also found a bold solution for the city transport problem in London's Underground railway. At huge cost, only managed with American financial help, electrical systems replaced the dirty steam underground trains and new lines were tunnelled. The 'Tube' proved to be the quickest and cheapest way to cross London: 37,000 passengers travelled on the first day of the Bakerloo Line in 1906. The moving staircase, the escalator, was a sensation at Earl's Court Station in 1911; its safety was demonstrated by a nimble man with a wooden leg.

Middle class life
The suburban commuter trains brought shoppers to town later in the day. Shopping was changing. Retailers like Lipton's or Sainsbury's in the food industry, had chains of shops and their own branded goods. An Edwardian innovation was the 'big store' that transformed London's Oxford Street. Gordon Selfridge had learned in Chicago's Marshall Field store how to sell many products under one roof. He opened his London store in 1909. 'This is not a shop; it is a social centre', claimed Selfridge. 'In my store, women can realize some of their dreams.'

City suburbs were divided by keenly-observed gradations of class. The lower middle-class office workers, whose numbers had risen as demands for office skills developed, occupied the inner suburbs. They struggled to maintain standards on inadequate incomes, fearing the rising power of the working class whose 'tumbled tenements' they commuted through each day, 'dimly distrustful', wrote Masterman, 'of the forces fermenting in this uncouth laboratory'. By day, these inner suburbs still echoed to the old street cries, the muffin man and his bell, or the magic of the organ-grinder's tunes.

New electric underground railway lines were opened in London during the Edwardian era. They provided a swift, cheap way to cross the city.

SANCTUARY.

" 'Tis pleasant, through the loopholes of retreat,
To peep at such a world; to see the stir
Of the great Babel, and not feel the crowd;
To hear the roar she sends through all her gates
At a safe distance, where the dying sound
Falls a soft murmur on th' uninjured ear."
William Cowper.

The Strand *was an outstanding magazine of the time, in which the* Sherlock Holmes *stories first appeared.*

In the outer suburbs lived the professional middle classes with interesting work, adequate incomes and leisure time. Contemporary novelists like E. M. Forster mocked the respectable life of these suburbans, but they had a real culture. It was a great age of reading. In the drawing room, beside the admirable story-magazines like the *Strand*, in which Sherlock Holmes first appeared, lay new cheap reprints of popular books, such as Collins Classics and Everyman's Library – heralding a revolution in publishing. It was a golden age of children's writing, too, with J. M. Barrie's *Peter Pan*, E. Nesbit's *The Railway Children* and Kenneth Grahame's *The Wind in the Willows*. The piano remained important in providing evenings of home-made music, while the phonograph, with its cylinder records, and gramophone, with discs, were becoming popular. For the young, the rhythms of the American-led 'rag time' craze after 1912 were the beginnings of the popular music revolution.

The Edwardian home tended to be less cluttered and brighter than its Victorian counterpart. The new simplicity, shown in Heal's catalogue, attacked 'pretentious stuffiness'. In 1908, the *Daily Mail* Ideal Home Exhibition was launched. Here the latest domestic gadgets were displayed: electric fires and kettles, gas cookers, primitive steam washing machines. The vacuum cleaner was now small enough to carry round the house. The use of the telephone was transforming social intercourse.

Country life

The countryside of Edwardian Britain, lovingly described by Edward Thomas in his poems and essays, was still exquisite. Wild flowers made carpets of glory on the verges of winding lanes, disturbed only by the occasional cyclist or pony and trap. There were remote areas virtually unchanged since Stuart times. By 1910, motor cars were shattering the peace, throwing up grey dust to ruin hedges and cottage gardens. What E. M. Forster called the 'red rust' of suburbia followed.

A depression in agriculture, created by the flood of imported food after 1875, had caused rural decay. Prices, notably for cereals, had fallen. Only particular products, like milk, carried swiftly into towns by improved transport, remained really profitable. By 1914, Britain was importing half its food.

The fall in land prices brought changes of ownership. Death duties (1894) and land taxes (1909) hastened change: nineteen noble estates were up for sale in 1912. Tenant farmers had more independence, following the Agricultural Holdings Acts between 1875 and 1908. At the bottom of the social scale, the old cry that labourers should be given allotments of land was revived: a Smallholdings Act of 1908 empowered Local Authorities to buy land for this use.

The agricultural depression also caused people to leave rural areas. The wages and status of the farm labourer were low; even rural Trade Unionism, revived at this time in East Anglia, could not help. In his survey, *Rural England*, Sir Henry Rider Haggard concerned himself with the drift to the towns. 'Some parts of England are become almost as lonesome as the veld of Africa ... People are deserting the villages wholesale, leaving behind them the mentally incompetent and the physically unfit.' The fate of the countryman in the city was often unhappy. Haggard met such a man weeping in the Strand: his family was 'learning by sharp experience the meaning of the word starvation'.

The state of workers' housing was also criticized. The cottage was too often a rural slum, condemned by investigators like Seebohm Rowntree, whose book, *How the Labourer Lives*, was written to support Lloyd George's pre-war campaign for reform in the countryside.

Motor cars shattered the peace of country villages. This runaway car, throwing up dust and scattering children and hens, depicts the problems.

An enormous breakfast was a feature of the long weekend at the Edwardian country house.

Contemporaries also regretted the decay in old skills and traditions. Cecil Sharp was just able to record the English heritage of folk song before it disappeared. George Sturt wrote about crafts like those in his own wheelwright's shop: the machine was destroying them. The appearance of the tractor was to bring the end of the farm horse. Sentimental rebels against technology tried to stem the tide: the 'Simple Life Press' preached 'the restoration of country life in place of that of the modern manufacturing town'.

The countryside was still a playground for some of the rich. The long weekend at the great country house was a characteristic Edwardian social event. Vita Sackville-West recalled Knole House in Kent: 'All was warmth and security . . . The grey walls, the flag on the tower, the verdure of the trees, and hares and deer feeding in the glades . . . Down in the garden on a lawn of brilliant green, the sprinkled figures . . . their laughter and the tap of croquet mallets . . .' Guests brought mountains of luggage, as each phase of the weekend demanded elaborate changes of clothes. There was lavish food. The fabulous Edwardian breakfast

29

Guests at a house party enjoy a picnic at a Devon and Somerset stag hunt meeting. Hunting was a typical leisure pursuit for the wealthy.

was typical. Lady Cynthia Asquith remembered how 'the little blue flames under the array of lidded, silver chafing dishes kept piping hot the crisp, curly bacon, eggs (poached, boiled and fried), ... haddock, swimming in melted butter ... Porridge immersed in thick yellow cream.' The careful hierarchy of the guests was echoed 'below stairs', where visiting servants were carefully fitted into the pattern of precedence, stretching from the majestic butler and housekeeper down to the 'tweeny', or between maid, who did odd jobs. These country houses with their army of servants were like self-contained villages. The work, in the over-furnished interiors and with the coal-burning fires and kitchen-ranges, was hard: even the master's small change was washed and his newspaper ironed. This was the last age of servants. The 1914 Census counted 1.25 million people so employed, but that number declined sharply after 1918.

The Great War was to speed the end of the country house. H. G. Wells wrote in 1909: 'The great houses stand in the parks still, the cottages cluster respectfully on their borders, too ... The English countryside persists obstinately in looking what it was. It is like an early day in a fine October. The hand of change rests on it all, unfelt, unseen ... before it grips and ends the thing for ever ...'

4 MASS COMMUNICATIONS, LEISURE AND THE ARTS

The Edwardian era saw a rapid development of the mass media revolution that began at the end of the nineteenth century.

Newspapers and advertising

The rise of the popular, large circulation newspaper depended on various developments coming together: printing technology that could now produce thousands of copies an hour; the spread of mass education that had created a new audience; and the growth of advertising which kept the papers cheap.

Advertising became a feature of mass urban society. This famous brand of custard powder is advertised in a magazine.

CUSTARD WITH FRUIT

Copyright.

Nature provides the fruit:
"BIRD" supplies the custard:
Try them together.

BIRD'S CUSTARD POWDER

Alfred Harmsworth (later Lord Northcliffe) led the way. He had become rich with a popular magazine, *Answers*, aimed at 'the great new generation that is being turned out by the board schools'. In 1896, Harmsworth began the *Daily Mail*, the 'busy man's daily journal', intended for the lower middle-class market. To make his papers sell, he used the same techniques as the American pioneer of journalism, William Randolph Hearst used in his million-circulation *New York Journal*.

In the *Daily Mail* instruction was to be mixed with entertainment. The paper was to 'make life more pleasant, more entertaining for the average man'. News reports were brief: Harmsworth's message to his writers was explain, simplify, clarify. Talking points – the flying machine, the German menace, the Naval Race – ran beside actual news. There was plenty of coverage of sport and movements in the women's world. During the Boer War, the *Daily Mail* reached the magic million circulation mark. Harmsworth started the *Daily Mirror* in 1903, as the first paper to use half-tone photographs, and later bought

Football became a new passion for city workers. This 1907 cup final between Everton and Sheffield Wednesday attracted 84,000 spectators.

Boating on the Thames was a typical Edwardian relaxation. Notice the maids brought along to serve the meals.

and revitalized the *Times*. Harmsworth had his rivals: Arthur Pearson's *Daily Express* pioneered Hearst-style headlines on the front page. These new popular papers had a wide influence on popular public opinion in the years before the Great War.

Newspapers were covered in advertising: nine successive days of whole page splashes, heralding the opening of Selfridge's store, appeared in the *Daily Mail* in 1909, for example. Advertising was another feature of mass urban society, borrowed from American commerce. The famous brand names – Pear's soap, Player's cigarettes, Bovril – were everywhere, poster hoardings being one of the few colourful aspects of grey Edwardian cities. The dishonesty and slick style of the new advertising, with its 'lies and clamour', were satirized by H. G. Wells in his novel *Tono-Bungay*.

Sport and holidays

Leisure and entertainment was also changing. After the Factory Act of 1867, some workers now had Saturday afternoon free, and an enthusiasm for soccer developed, encouraged by journalists and better public transport which allowed people to get to matches. Fans saw their local teams grow from waste-ground or park players into professional teams. The crowd coming to London for the big match was a novelty: at the 1901 Crystal Palace Cup Final there were 110,820 spectators and the capital seemed to some to be invaded by 'cloth-capped hordes, northern-voiced, thick-suited, heavy-booted'.

The 1908 Olympic Games in London; the marathon runner, Italian Pietri Dorando, was helped across the finishing line and disqualified.

Traditional interests continued. The Derby and the Oxford-Cambridge Boat Race were great national events. Cricket drew huge crowds in its 'Golden Age', to watch C. B. Fry, 'as handsome and superbly-made as a Greek god', who captained England and was offered the throne of Albania! Golf and tennis became Edwardian passions, and courses and courts spread rapidly in the outer suburbs. The Olympic Games, held at the White City, London, were a highlight of 1908. Britain, with the largest team, won most gold medals in a strange array of events. The dense crowds lining the marathon course – in which the leader, Italian Pietri Durando, was dramatically

The Edwardian seaside; bathing machines, sunshades and people wearing thick clothes on the seafront at Hastings.

disqualified after being helped across the finishing line – were a portent of the later twentieth century's passion for international sport.

Industrial employers only gradually accepted the idea that holidays were beneficial for workers. The Bank Holiday of 1871 gave hard-pressed employees days that H. G. Wells's Mr Polly called 'diamonds among pebbles'. By 1911, the Trades Union Congress was demanding proper paid holidays for all workers. Poor families in London went hop-picking. Jack London watched them and exclaimed: 'They resemble some vile spawn from underground ... their very presence is an outrage to the fresh bright sun and green and growing things'. Wealthier

Hop-picking in Kent was a traditional working holiday for families from London's East End.

workers enjoyed a holiday by the sea. Resorts, popular in Victoria's reign, spread their suburbs across the cliffs and downs. Beaches were alive with music from German bands, or the elegant pierrot shows that were replacing the old minstrel shows. Clumsy bathing machines, from which women discreetly swam, still trundled to the sea-edge, but mixed bathing was an Edwardian innovation.

Music hall, cinema and theatre

In the cities, music hall was enjoying a final heyday. It had grown from the singing room of the Victorian working-class tavern to become the variety theatre, where the great stars like Marie Lloyd, Harry Lauder or George Robey could earn a thousand pounds a week, going from one theatre to another by cab. From the halls came tunes which set the whole country singing. Songs such as *It's a long way to Tipperary*, first heard in 1913, became the poignant marching songs of the British Army in the Great War.

The 'moving pictures' of the 'cinematograph' eventually killed the music halls, having at first been just a part of their programmes. The first purpose-built cinema opened at Colne, Lancashire in 1908. By 1914,

These were the last great days of the music hall. Here Dan Leno plays to a packed London audience.

Charlie Chaplin began his career in the London music hall, before rising to become a star of the cinema.

there were 3,500 provided by astute businessmen. English cameramen filmed news items such as Queen Victoria's funeral or daily life in the streets and Derby days. These films are now amongst the most moving documents of Edwardian life. The first story films, like the American *Great Train Robbery*, delighted audiences. Cecil Hepworth's *Rescued by Rover* was so popular that all the prints were worn out through over-use and it had to be reshot. The American comedies of Charlie Chaplin clinched the success of the 'poor man's theatre': significantly he began his career in the London music hall. The benefit of the cinema was noted by a contemporary: 'The masses spend less on drink and more on drama. The national habits are changing. Recent years have seen the rise of amusement and in some way, too, of culture.'

The middle classes despised the cinema. They preferred the theatre. There they could enjoy contrasts: the old Victorian melodramatic-style Shakespeare, or the bold, progressive stage designs for fashionable musical comedy, or even the instructive plays of George Bernard Shaw and Harley Granville Barker. Shaw thought the theatre should deal with important social issues: 'Modern civilization is rapidly multiplying the class to which theatre is both school and church'. The censor mutilated some of the greatest work of the time. At the end of the period, the jazz review *Hello Ragtime* dazzled young Edwardians, as did the visiting Russian ballet, which the poet Rupert Brooke saw fifteen times!

The arts and science
In the literary world, Victorian giants like Rudyard Kipling and Henry James had already done their best work. Thomas Hardy had finished with novels but produced some of his greatest poems in these years. H. G. Wells abandoned science fiction and wrote Edwardian classics like *Kipps*, *Tono-Bungay* and *Mr Polly*. His *Ann Veronica*, about women's rights, aroused a storm and was refused by libraries. *Howard's End* by E. M. Forster now seems a profound study of the values of Edwardian society.

Poetry enjoyed new popularity after the publication of Edward Marsh's best-selling collections of *Georgian Poetry*, from 1911 onwards. Marsh's friend, Rupert Brooke, the Cambridge poet, was to become very famous when his death coincided with the publication of his war sonnets.

English music produced a burst of creativity. What other Europeans called 'the land without music' produced a genius, Sir Edward Elgar. Edwardians liked his *Pomp and Circumstance* marches and *Land of Hope and Glory* seemed the expression of Imperial grandeur, reflecting, said Elgar, 'a nation with great military proclivities'. English music was gently progressive, unlike that of the European avant-garde: Igor Stravinsky's *Rite of Spring* caused a riot when first played in fashionable Paris in 1913.

Interest in the art world centred on the attacks by conservatives on the new art, above all on the sculpture of Jacob Epstein, whose figures made to decorate a London building were described in 1908 as 'a form of statuary which no careful father would wish his daughter to see'. To most Edwardians, art meant the realistic painting shown each year at the Royal Academy. Roger Fry's Post-Impressionist art exhibition raised a chorus of ridicule and anger. Reporters wrote of 'intolerable

Edward Elgar was the outstanding Edwardian composer. His music expressed the imperialistic mood of pre-war Britain.

and outrageous rubbish'. Gauguin was 'weird and uncouth'; Matisse and Cézanne 'parade their incapacity'; Van Gogh was 'an unhappy madman', his work an 'exhibition of a diseased mind'. The stress of the years before 1914 was reflected in the Italian Futurist artists, who worshipped speed, the machine and war. 'All beauty is based on strife' they proclaimed in a manifesto. They were imitated by a group of English artists called vorticists, whose magazine *Blast* appeared in 1914.

The most significant of all British creative effort came in the sciences, where the studies of Ernest Rutherford and J. J. Thomson, exploring radioactivity and the structure of the atom, laid the foundations of modern atomic physics and of the nuclear age. Enough was known of the implications of their work for H. G. Wells to write, in 1914, *The World Set Free*, a science fiction story of a future European war, in which atomic bombs are dropped from aeroplanes.

40

5 POLITICAL PREOCCUPATIONS: AT HOME

The Edwardian era saw some important reforms passed through Parliament. It was also marked by the beginning of a revolution in the distribution of political power in Britain.

Balfour's Conservatives

The uneasy Conservative government of A. J. Balfour produced the outstanding Education Act of 1902 which ended late Victorian educational confusion. Local Education Authorities, based on County and Borough Councils, replaced the old School Boards that had been responsible for state elementary schooling since the 1870 Act. In addition, LEA's were empowered to create state secondary schools. Although the new 'grammar schools' were fee-paying (until 1907 when some free place scholarships were granted), the Act did increase the opportunities for boys and, especially, girls, offering a ladder to reach university. Balfour boldly confronted the 'religious difficulty' that had hindered English schooling. The private 'voluntary' schools, funded by

Mass drill in a school playground, in 1906. There was much concern about the physical condition of children at this time.

the various churches, were now to be given financial assistance from local rates. This caused resentment for years, especially from non-conformists, who objected to supporting the schools of other churches, particularly those of the Catholics: 'Rome on the rates'.

Balfour was less fortunate with other domestic policies. The controversy over 'tariff reform', begun by Joseph Chamberlain, divided the Conservative party. Since becoming Colonial Secretary in 1895, Chamberlain had wanted to see the scattered parts of the British Empire more closely tied together by an economic union. In a speech at Birmingham in May 1903, Chamberlain proposed a system of Imperial preference. Tariffs (or duties charged) on goods exchanged between Britain and the Empire would be lowered, while those on imports from other countries would be raised. Greatly increased Imperial trade would, he said, 'make the British Empire powerful and influential for good beyond the dreams of anyone now living'.

Joseph Chamberlain speaking on Tariff reform in Birmingham in 1903. He was answering the case that his proposal would mean more expensive bread.

VOTE FOR

Home Rule.

Democratic Government.

ıstice to Labour

₁o Monopoly.

o Landlordism

Temperance Reform.

Healthy Homes.

Fair Rents.

Eight-Hour Day.

Work for the Unemployed.

KEIR HARDIE.

An election poster for James Keir-Hardie, who became leader of the Labour Party after its first great success at the 1906 General Election.

There was intense interest in the speech from all sides. Opponents could see that tariff reform would end Britain's long-held policy of free trade, which brought in cheap food imports for the cities. The Liberals were delighted by the divisions among Conservatives, and began to talk of the 'dearer loaf', which trade barriers would bring. On the day after the Birmingham speech, the future Liberal leader, Herbert Asquith, wrote to his wife: 'Wonderful news today and it is only a question of time when we shall sweep the country'.

The 1906 Election
When the Conservatives resigned office, the General Election of 1906 did indeed give the Liberals a landslide victory. They were to be one of the great reforming governments of this century. David Lloyd George, their rising political star, predicted 'a new order coming from the people

43

Crowds celebrated Joseph Chamberlain's return at Birmingham, after the dramatic election of 1906, although he had split the Conservative Party allowing the Liberals to win.

of this country. It is a quiet but certain revolution'. Balfour sourly detected in the election result 'a faint echo' of the 1905 uprisings in Russia.

The twenty-nine Labour M.P.s were a particular sensation. Labour, said Balfour, was 'a new planet, suddenly introduced into our political heavens'. After the 1892 election, which saw the Scottish Socialist leader, James Keir Hardie enter Parliament wearing his cloth cap, Trades Union Congress and left-wing groups combined to form the Labour Representation Committee (LRC) to support the election of more socialist M.P.s. Their great success came in 1906; then they became the Labour Party, with Keir Hardie as chairman and James Ramsey Macdonald – who became the first Labour Prime Minister in 1924 – as Secretary. The introduction of payment for M.P.s in 1911 made the future of the Party secure.

The Liberals were indebted to Labour for help during the campaign. Labour therefore had some influence over government policy. Moreover, as one commentator noted, 'what may be called the spirit of socialism pervades the whole House'. Socialist thinking coloured the first Liberal reforms: the School Meals Act (1906), allowing LEA's to give free dinners to poor children, and the Act of 1907 that enforced medical inspection of school pupils. Both measures were reactions to the work of the Committee on Physical Deterioration.

Liberal social reforms included the compulsory medical inspection of schoolchildren after 1907. Here children are being treated for head lice.

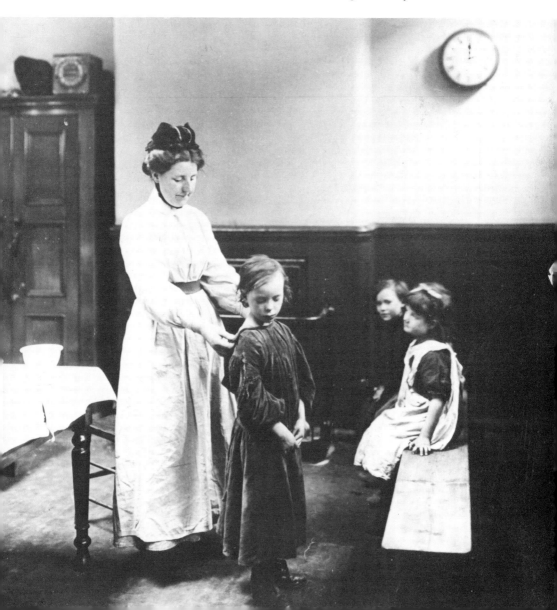

Old Age Pensions were introduced in 1909, bringing much needed help to poor people over seventy years old.

In 1908 came the introduction of Old Age Pensions, for people aged over seventy who had no other income. The pensions were not generous (25 pence a week for single people; 38 pence for married couples) but they were what the Chancellor, Lloyd George, described as a 'real beginning' in that they relieved the elderly from the humiliations of the Poor Law. When the pension was first given out in 1909, Flora Thompson, in *Lark Rise to Candleford*, remembered the delight of old people in her Oxfordshire village: 'At first when they went to the Post Office to draw it, tears of gratitude would run down the cheeks of some and they would say as they picked up the money, "God bless that Lord George ...".'

Asquith's reforming government

When Asquith took over from Sir Henry Campbell-Bannermann as Prime Minister in 1908, the pace of reform quickened. Asquith set free the talents of his brilliant Ministers, Lloyd George, and Winston Churchill, then President of the Board of Trade. These two put together the National Insurance Act of 1911. Financial help was to be given by the state to the sick and unemployed. Compulsory payments were to be made weekly by employers and employees, and supplemented by state funds drawn from taxation. Lloyd George, who had risen from a humble background himself, explained the purpose of the measures: 'I can see now the humble homes of the people with the dark clouds of anxiety, disease, distress, privation hanging heavily over them. And I see, again, another vision. . . . The Old Age Pension Act, the National Insurance Act . . . descending like breezes from the hills of my native land . . . and clearing the gloom away until the rays of God's sun have pierced the narrowest window.'

The government's plans to raise money to support these reforms won Lloyd George the cartoon reputation as the 'Philanthropic Highwayman', robbing the rich to pay the poor. His 'People's Budget' of 1909 – 'to wage implacable war against poverty and squalidness' – brought on the constitutional battle between the Liberal government and the Conservative-dominated House of Lords. Income tax was raised to six pence in the pound, with allowances for earned (but not

Winston Churchill was one of the Liberal Government's outstanding ministers. Here, as First Lord of the Admiralty, he inspects a Naval Guard of Honour.

unearned) income and for children. Supertax of two pence in the pound was introduced for those with large incomes. Unearned profit from land was taxed, and death duties were raised. Cars and petrol were taxed for the first time.

Commons versus the Lords
The Budget charges seem to us modest enough but they aroused bitter opposition in 1909, as they struck most at the rich. Conservatives saw this as 'vindictive' and landowners condemned it as 'the beginning of the end of all rights of property'. After furious debate in the Commons, the Lords, sensationally, voted to reject the Bill. The House of Lords was dominated by Conservatives whose leader, Balfour, had, in the face of the huge Liberal majority, persuaded his colleagues there to try 'thwarting and distorting' government policy by altering or rejecting their

The Chancellor, David Lloyd George, seen as the 'Philanthropic Highwayman', taking from the rich to pay Social Security to the poor.

Herbert Asquith became Prime Minister in 1908. He introduced important reforms and led the battle of Commons against Lords.

Bills. Lloyd George contemptuously described the Lords as 'Balfour's poodle – it fetched and carried for him, barked at and bit anybody he set it into. That was the great revising Chamber . . .'

In a powerful speech, Asquith condemned the Lords: 'The absolute veto which it at present possesses must go.' He had only one course of action: to appeal to the electorate on the theme, 'Who governs the country?' In January 1910, having won a narrow majority, Asquith brought forward a Parliamentary Bill: firstly, the Lords should never again reject a Budget; secondly, any Bill could only be delayed for two years by the Lords. The Peers hastily passed the 1909 Budget and put forward their own proposals for reform. A conference of representatives of the two political parties discussed the issues but failed to reach agreement, causing a second election to be called in December, 1910. Again the Liberals just managed to win a majority. The coronation of the new King, George V, delayed the debates on the Parliament Bill until July 1911. Asquith warned Balfour that he had discovered, with the King's consent, a solution to the crisis. This 'understanding' was revealed to a packed and stifling House of Lords on 9 August. If the Bill failed to pass, the King had agreed to create 249 new Liberal Peers to give Asquith a majority in the Upper House. Opposition now collapsed: the Lords finally passed the Bill and agreed to the extinction of their absolute veto. Lord Curzon gloomily saw the change as 'a revolution greater than any since the Civil War'. Any British government now only needed a majority in the Commons for its measures to pass into law.

6 POLITICAL PREOCCUPATIONS: ABROAD

Britain's overseas possessions and Dominions, acquired almost casually in, it was said, 'a fit of absence of mind' as the result of commercial and military struggles with other European countries, made up the largest Empire ever known, with a population of some 416 million. It was also the most widespread, with key bases like Malta and Gibraltar allowing the Royal Navy to protect its trade routes. There were the former white colonies – the Dominions of Canada and New Zealand, and the Commonwealth of Australia. India, a vast subcontinent of three hundred million people, 'the brightest jewel in the Empire's crown', was still largely under direct British rule, although the pressures for independence had already begun. Egypt, vital for control of the Suez Canal, was administered by Britain, as was Sudan, conquered in 1898. The European 'scramble for Africa', following the

British Imperialism in India; a British official is attended by Indian servants. One holds a large fan to keep his master cool.

The Boer War; a stylized view of Imperial Yeomanry attacking a Boer post near Bethlehem in the Orange River Colony, 1901.

opening up of the continent by explorers and missionaries, had brought Britain huge new territories – the Gold Coast, Nigeria, Kenya, Uganda and Zanzibar – more, at this stage, for prestige than for profit.

The notion of Britain as an Imperial power had attracted little interest at home until the late nineteenth century produced a fever of nationalism in Europe. The Golden and Diamond Jubilees of Queen Victoria in 1887 and 1897 had therefore been great Imperial occasions that emphasized Britain's power and pride.

The Boer War and after
South Africa had, however, brought a crisis in British Imperialism. The British had settled in the Cape in 1806, driving Dutch colonists, the Boers, inland. When gold and diamonds were discovered in the Boer 'republics', Orange Free State and Transvaal, the British tried to seize control of these territories. Hostility became actual conflict in 1880. A second, more serious Boer War began in 1899. After initial disasters, a large British force finally broke the Boers in 1902, defeating their brilliant guerrilla tactics by a 'scorched earth' policy that destroyed Boer settlements and interned their women and children in the world's first concentration camps.

The British Army's use of barbed wire and concentration camps eventually defeated the Boer guerrilla tactics.

A permanent settlement of South Africa was a major concern of Conservative and Liberal politicians in Britain. In 1909, the British colonies of Cape and Natal joined the former Boer republics to form the Union of South Africa. In their anxiety for reconciliation with the Boer leaders, and to make secure the sea route round the Cape, Liberal negotiators left one fatal flaw in the agreement: non-whites in the Boer states were not given the vote. From this deadly seed sprang, forty years later, the policy of 'apartheid' or separate development for blacks and whites. J. A. Hobson, in *The Crisis of Liberalism*, looked forward to the South African conflicts of our own time: 'Deliberately to set out upon a new career as a civilized nation with a definition of civilization which takes as the criterion race and colour ... is nothing else than to sow a crop of dark and dangerous problems for the future.'

The Boer War created many doubts about British Imperialism and a debate continued to 1914. To some thinkers, the Empire had been exposed as a racket, that benefited only a few businessmen, who used the Union Jack as 'the greatest commercial asset in the world'. Capital, drawn to investments abroad, might be better used to 'colonize' England by helping the poor at home. On the other side, propagandists saw the Empire as a mission of the 'superior' European to civilize the undeveloped world, as Churchill said: 'to administer justice where all was violence ... to draw the riches from the soil ... to increase in whole peoples their capacity for pleasure'. It was in this spirit that Empire Day (24 May) was celebrated from 1906 onwards. Even at his Salford slum school, Robert Roberts remembered his teachers training children to 'think Imperially' as they proudly contemplated the red British areas on the world map. Some politicians wanted the Empire to be more closely united, so that Britain – 'the weary Titan that staggers under the too vast orb of its fate', as Joseph Chamberlain remarked – could share Imperial defence and development with the rising Dominions. Others preferred the idea of a looser federation of 'units in a greater unity': the notion of the 'Commonwealth' was first raised at this time.

The end of 'splendid isolation'
The Boer War briefly united the European powers against Britain. In view of this, the late Victorian policy of 'splendid isolation' began to seem less attractive. After 1902, Britain began to look for new alliances.

Bismarck's creation, after 1871, of a German Federal Empire from the patchwork of small German states had altered the balance of power in Europe. A Dual Alliance of Germany and the Austro-Hungarian Empire had been joined in 1882 by the newly-unified Italy. The Central Powers as they were known, feared Russia and France, who agreed on an alliance in 1894. These so-called defensive alliances were dangerous because they entailed plans for automatic mobilization (the calling up

King Edward VII, visiting Paris in 1903. He helped to improve relations with France, leading to the Entente Cordiale.

and movement of troops) in the event of a threat from an enemy. Mobilization could mean war because General Staff on both sides favoured the concept of the 'knock-out blow', a swift devastating military strike. There was already a cause for war in the Balkans, where Russia and Austria-Hungary disputed control over areas recently given up by the decaying Turkish Empire. This situation was summed up by William Watson, in his poem *The World in Armour* which imagined:

> The Europe of the present, as she stands
> Powerless from terror of her own vast power,
> And round her the sad kings, with sleepless hands,
> Piling the fagots, hour by doomful hour.

Fear of a Russian threat to British interests in the Far East made the Conservative government seek an alliance with Japan in 1902. This, in turn, drew Britain closer to Europe. As the 1904–5 war between Japan and Russia approached, France, anxious to avoid being drawn in, began to negotiate with Britain. Reconciliation between the old rivals was helped by Edward VII's popular visit to Paris in 1903. During the talks in London, France agreed to abandon interest in Egypt in return for recognition of her claims in Morocco. The agreement – the 'Entente Cordiale' – was signed in 1904. It was not an alliance but a promise of diplomatic support. Britain could still stand apart from future European conflicts.

The Moroccan crisis of 1905 tested and strengthened the 'Entente' and sharpened the temper of Anglo-German hostility. In March 1905, Kaiser Wilhelm II of Germany visited Tangier and declared that he saw Morocco as an independent country, where he would resent any interference in German interests. Fearing that Germany would obtain an Atlantic base for her new Navy, Britain supported France strongly at the Algeciras Conference of 1906. The Entente stood firm. Moreover, Britain and France began secret negotiations about military co-operation in the event of war. In 1907, Britain signed an Anglo-Russian Entente, which tried to settle disputes about the control of Persia.

Anglo-German rivalry

After 1905, Germany was seen as the most serious danger to Britain as a trade, colonial and military rival. From the turn of the century, the *Daily Mail* ran a campaign against the 'German menace'. A curious invasion mania sprang up, reflected in a spate of popular books, describing a German conquest of Britain: there were titles like *When William Came* or *The Enemy in our Midst*. Best known was the *Invasion of 1910* by William Le Queux, advertised by sandwich-board men dressed as Prussian soldiers. Best written was H. G. Wells's *The War in the Air*, describing the ruin of civilization after a German airship attack on the USA.

The first Dreadnought battleship, launched at Portsmouth in 1905, was a powerful and heavily-armed 'floating steel castle'.

Invasion mania was often linked with the campaign, run by the famous General, Lord Roberts, to introduce compulsory military service. This was resisted by the government, although the Army reforms of R. B. Haldane, Liberal Secretary of State for War, did reorganize the Army. An 'expeditionary force' was to be ready to move swiftly to the Continent in the event of war, and the Territorial Army of 300,000 part-time volunteers would help to deal with any invasion. The Navy would remain the main defence.

The naval 'race' was the centre of Anglo-German rivalry. The Germans had begun building a large Navy, as a symbol of national pride and ambition. A British tradition of supremacy at sea – whereby the Royal Navy was to have a strength equal to the combined strength of the next two largest rival fleets – now became a national obsession. 'To us, sea supremacy is a necessity of national life,' said Mr McKenna, First Sea Lord, in 1909. 'To Germany, it is a luxury of Imperial ambition. If we lost command of the sea, our commerce could be destroyed... She is playing for pride; we are playing for life – and we mean to win.'

The Naval Race between Britain and Germany seen as a game of poker. Britain tried to maintain a 60 per cent superiority over the German fleet.

Expenditure grew rapidly, especially after the powerful Dreadnought battleships, 'floating steel castles', entered service after 1906. Fears that Germany might be overtaking Britain raised the national cry, 'We want eight and we won't wait', the eight being new Dreadnoughts. 'We are not yet prepared to turn the face of every portrait of Nelson to the wall' commented the *Daily Telegraph*. Although some attempts at agreement with Germany to limit warship construction were made in 1912, the race continued, with Britain maintaining 60 per cent superiority.

A second Moroccan crisis in 1911, during which the Germans sent a gunboat to Agadir to demand territorial compensation from the French, bound Britain more closely to France. Military leaders concluded secret plans for wartime co-operation. British troops would be sent to defend France. The British fleet would defend the Atlantic and the North Sea, while the French concentrated on the Mediterranean.

European tensions continued to grow after 1912. 'The situation is extra-ordinary' wrote an American observer to his President. 'It is militarism run stark mad ... There is some day to be an awful cataclysm. There is too much hatred, too many jealousies.'

56

7 DIRECT ACTION: CHALLENGES TO PARLIAMENT

The Liberals' second term of office after 1910 was marked by social and political turmoil, as 'direct action' – from Trade Unions, from suffragettes, and from supporters or opponents of Irish Home Rule – was used to challenge the rule of Parliament.

Trade Unions and strikes
The Trades Union Congress, which first met in 1868, had been relatively mild-mannered at the turn of the century, restrained by unemployment which was high between 1901 and 1905. However, clumsy handling of test cases by the Law Lords had been much resented. Thus the Taff Vale decision of 1901, following a Welsh railway dispute, had made unions liable for damage caused by strike action, although the Liberals' Trades Disputes Act of 1906 over-rode this verdict. The Osborne judgement of

Trade Union direct action increased rapidly after 1908. Here troops and police move to confront dockers in Liverpool in 1911.

1909 was also clumsy: it was declared illegal for unions to support a political party from their funds. Unions became embittered: wealth and the law seemed combined against them. Membership grew rapidly, from two to four million between 1901 and 1913.

There were also economic reasons for the chaos after 1910. Wages had not kept pace with prices inflated by the flood of South African gold. Better technology was making old skilled trades obsolete. Mass education had produced a more thoughtful worker, who, as H. G. Wells noted in *What the Worker Wants*, 'reads, talks, has general ideas and a sense of the round world'. He could see what a Labour M.P. called the 'spectacle of leisured luxury' and he wanted a greater share of this prosperity. After 1910, when an economic boom reduced unemployment, the unions tried, by the 'direct action' of the strike, to win better pay and conditions.

Strike fever grew apace. Whereas between 1901 and 1907, lost working days ranged between one and four million a year, after 1908, the average was ten or eleven. 1911, with forty-one million days lost, was the blackest year of all. Causes of strikes were the mere symptoms of deep-seated grievances. Inadequate government processes to settle disputes allowed trouble to fester. Serious disruption began in the hot summer of 1911, 'a strange hectic period of our economic history', as the prominent union leader, Ben Tillett, called it. In Wales, men of the Miners' Federation had been on strike for ten months. At Tonypandy, a miner was shot dead by police; two more rioters were killed by troops at Llanelli. Two dockers were shot in Liverpool, where troops were

Violence during the long Welsh mining strike of 1910–11. Troops with fixed bayonets moved against rioters at Llanelli; two were killed.

Mounted police escorting milk carts past militant dock strikers who tried to prevent the delivery of milk in Liverpool.

repulsed by stone-throwing mobs. August brought the first national rail strike, which lasted two days at the height of the holiday season. 1912 proved equally bad. There was a four month national coal strike, which succeeded in winning pay increases, followed by severe but ineffective trouble from port-workers in London. During the heat of August, wrote the historian, George Dangerfield, 'everything began to die ... vegetables and flour grew scarcer and scarcer; great piles of fruit lay perishing in the docks ... famine grew nearer hour by hour'. The politician Austen Chamberlain felt that 'the whole machinery of national life was slowly stopping'. He feared more violence, noting that a gun shop he knew of had sold its entire stock of revolvers.

The eventual failure of the dock strikes in London showed the unions that they must organize themselves more effectively. From the USA, British Unionism tried to imitate the example, given by the massive American Federation of Labour, that large unions were more effective. The railwaymen led the way, combining to form the National Union of Railwaymen in 1913. Another influence came from France where the revolutionary doctrine of 'syndicalism' had had much influence. By this theory, great national unions would be formed that would seize control of industry, destroying capitalist owners. Syndicalism was evident in a 1912 pamphlet, produced in Wales, called *The Miners' Next Step*. It promised 'drastic and militant action' leading to a general strike. Right-wing opinion was horrified: a Conservative M.P. spoke of 'incitement to mutiny'.

The first national railway strike in August, 1911. Here strikers march past Willesden station in London.

Both sides were exaggerating. Edwardian trade disputes were, in fact, fairly ineffective and usually only managed to hurt workers in other industries. The so-called 'Triple Alliance' of miners, railwaymen and port-workers, proposed at the miners' conference of 1913, whereby action was to be co-ordinated, was more a policy of consultation than the revolutionary 'next step'. However, the rail strike, planned for November 1914, might have put the government to severe test. Sir George Askwith, a leading industrial conciliator, forecast in 1913 'movements in this country coming to a head of which recent events have been a small foreshadowing'. The outbreak of war postponed the workers' crisis to the General Strike of 1926.

Votes for women

Since the mid-nineteenth century, middle-class women had won important victories in the struggle for more independence. The New Woman had more freedom in Edwardian society. She had a better education. There were more job opportunities for her: in medicine, teaching, shops and offices. She might be a 'typewriter' or switchboard girl.

Yet complete emancipation was still remote. 'The cage is enlarged' wrote a journalist, 'but it is still a cage'. A woman's right to vote came to be a symbol of greater status and freedom. The various Reform Acts of the nineteenth century had left women without the suffrage. They could take part in local elections, but had otherwise to express their democratic wishes through their husbands. This argument had lost force. By 1913, there was a female population imbalance of over a million and many women were not marrying. Since 1870, there had been discussion of the issue in Parliament but nothing had been done.

Other countries had been more progressive in granting women the vote: New Zealand (1893), Australia (1902); newly-liberated Finland (1907) and Norway (1908). Certain American states also did so.

In 1897, the National Union of Women's Suffrage Societies (NUWSS) was formed by Mrs Garrett Fawcett. These 'suffragists' used orderly, constitutional methods to try to win 'votes for ladies'. In 1903, a more vigorous militant group broke away, led by Emmeline Pankhurst. Christened 'suffragettes' by the *Daily Mail*, they formed the Women's Social and Political Union (WSPU). Its object was 'immediate enfranchisement' by political action. The election campaign of 1906 marked the start of militancy. The interruption of politicians' speeches, the arrest and imprisonment of Christabel Pankhurst, Emmeline's daughter, gave the cause sensational publicity.

After the failure of Private Members' Bills, concerned with female suffrage, in 1907–8, militant action increased. Hundreds of women tried to enter Parliament. Some chained themselves to the railings round the House, or to the grille of the Ladies' Gallery. Two women had themselves posted to 10 Downing Street as parcels. Others burnt the slogan 'votes for women' with acid on to a Birmingham golf course. In 1908, 13,000 women bearing the green, purple and white colours of the suffragettes, assembled in Hyde Park.

Mr Asquith remained stubborn. Worried for his delicate Parliamentary majority after 1910, he was not displeased when a Reform Bill,

A suffragette procession in London, in June 1911, protesting against the imprisonment of women who were fighting for the vote.

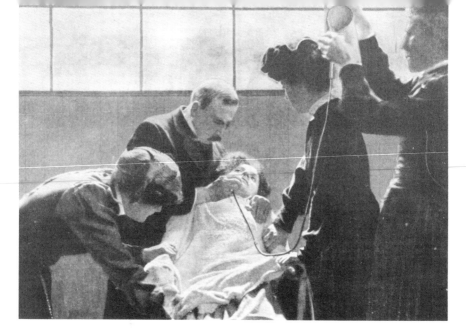

Forcible feeding of a suffragette hunger striker in prison. Liquid food was poured down a flexible tube through the nose into the stomach.

that virtually promised women the vote, foundered on a technicality in 1912. Mrs Pankhurst claimed that 'war is declared on women' and promised to use the 'time-honoured argument of the stone'. In spectacular attacks, relays of women smashed shop windows in London.

In 1913, the movement found a martyr, when Emily Davison hurled herself to her death under the King's horse at the Derby. Another woman recalled 'an awful silence ... then suddenly many cries and shouts arose as people swarmed out onto the racecourse. I was rooted with horror until a man snatched the paper I was holding in my hand (a copy of *The Suffragette*) and beat it across my face'. The funeral became a great feminist parade, as a guard of honour, dressed in white with purple sashes, led 6,000 women mourners.

When women in prison went on hunger strike, they were held down and forcibly fed. A rubber tube was thrust down nostril or throat. Sylvia Pankhurst described how 'the pain was like having the teeth drawn ... I was struggling madly to stiffen my muscles and close my throat. They got it down – at last they said "that's all" and I vomited the tube up ...' This barbaric treatment was stopped after protest in Parliament. The notorious 'Cat and Mouse' Act came in 1913. Those on hunger strike were released until they recovered: then they were re-arrested.

The campaign of violence reached a feverish climax in 1914. 'Danger-duty' volunteers set fire to remote, empty buildings. A small bomb was placed on the Coronation Chair in Westminster Abbey. The King himself came under pressure. Girls addressed him through megaphones

THE CAT AND MOUSE ACT

PASSED BY THE LIBERAL GOVERNMENT

THE LIBERAL CAT
ELECTORS VOTE AGAINST HIM!
KEEP THE LIBERAL OUT!

Under this Act, hunger strikers were released but later re-arrested.

at the theatre. A debutante, at her presentation, shocked him by pleading 'stop this forcible feeding'. Mrs Pankhurst's deputation to the Palace was broken up by police and crowds of men, some of whom sported locks of women's hair in their buttonholes.

Mrs Emmeline Pankhurst was arrested during the suffragette attack on Buckingham Palace in May 1914.

The beginning of the war in 1914 changed everything. The two women's groups at once dedicated their energies to the national cause to such purpose that limited women's suffrage was granted in February 1918.

Irish Home Rule

The passing of the Parliament Act by the House of Lords in August 1911 revived the old Irish dream of escape from British domination. The election of December 1910 had left Asquith dependent on the goodwill of the Irish Nationalist M.P.s. To win their support, he had to introduce another Bill for Irish Home Rule.

Ireland had been bound to the rest of the United Kingdom by the Act of Union of 1800. For generations, the southern Irish had longed to break this knot. Irish independence was, however, a complex issue. Politicians before Asquith had tried to deal with the Irish problem. Gladstone, the late-Victorian Liberal leader, had tried unsuccessfully to pass Home Rule Bills in 1886 and 1892, splitting his party in the process. The complication was Ulster, the counties in the north-east of the island, settled three centuries before by Scottish Presbyterians. Ulster had, as a result, become very different to the Catholic South in religion, politics and economic structure. Religious antagonism was intense: to Ulster, Home Rule meant Rome rule. To them, that was intolerable and Ulstermen were ready to fight.

Asquith's Home Rule Bill was introduced in April 1912. It proposed limited self-rule with an Irish Parliament at Dublin, concerning itself with internal Irish affairs, while external matters were still handled by Westminster, where forty-two Irish Members were still to sit.

Sir Edward Carson speaking in 1912. He became the fierce leader of the Northern Irish in their campaign against Home Rule for Ireland.

The two sides, North and South, prepared for a struggle. The Irish Nationalists were led by John Redmond. To him, Home Rule had to include the whole island; otherwise extremist groups like Sinn Fein would demand complete Irish independence. Ulstermen were led by the dynamic Edward Carson, a leading barrister. In January 1913, Carson formed the Ulster Volunteers, a citizen's army, which contained 48,000 men by 1914. Wearing a badge marked 'For God and Ulster', they drilled and practised military tactics. In September, Carson invited the public to sign a 'solemn covenant', a pledge to 'defeat the present conspiracy to set up a Home Rule Parliament in Ireland'. Almost a quarter of a million Ulstermen signed it. The Southern response was to raise a force of Irish Nationalist Volunteers, who were advised to 'get a gun and do your part'. They were a hundred thousand strong by 1914, with many men coming from within Ulster itself.

Conservatives (who also proudly called themselves Unionists) supported Ulster. Their strength of hostility to the government was remarkable for an English opposition party. Their new leader, Andrew Bonar-Law, a Presbyterian from Glasgow, seemed to encourage the use of force. In a notorious speech Bonar-Law asserted that 'there are things stronger than Parliamentary majorities.' A British Covenant was signed by such famous right-wing figures as Lord Roberts, Edward Elgar and Rudyard Kipling.

The most unexpected resistance to Home Rule came from within the British Army. In March 1914, the government, anticipating an Ulster declaration of independence, decided to match Carson's threat of force with military strength. Winston Churchill, then First Lord of the

The fever of the Irish politics spreads to a new generation; boys imitate their elders by playing soldiers in Dublin, 1913.

Admiralty, described Carson in a speech as 'engaged in a treasonable conspiracy'. Two Army battalions in Ireland were ordered to move north against Ulster, and a squadron of battleships was sent to the Irish Sea. Many British officers had Ulster connections. A kind of mutiny therefore occurred at the Curragh barracks in Dublin. Fifty-seven officers chose to be dismissed rather than participate in military operations against Ulster.

Asquith hastily drew back. The military movements were suspended. New attempts at compromise were made, based on the partition of Ireland. In July 1914, the King called a conference at Buckingham Palace. Partition was not an easy solution: which exactly were the Ulster counties and where could a boundary run? No agreement was reached. Meanwhile, tensions in Ireland had been increased by gun-running operations. Thousands of rifles and rounds from Germany came ashore at Larne in the North in April, and, on 26 July, British troops intercepted a landing near Dublin for the Irish Volunteers: several people were killed and injured in the ensuing struggle. Civil war seemed inevitable.

The British Cabinet members were considering the problems of the Ulster border – what Churchill called 'the muddy by-ways of Fermanagh and Tyrone' – when they were told of Austria's ultimatum to Serbia, the first move towards European war. The Irish problem was set aside. The Home Rule Bill was passed in Parliament in September 1914, but its terms were postponed during wartime. More bitter episodes – the 1916 Easter Rising, and the civil war – were to make it inoperative, and to bring eventual partition and Southern Irish independence.

8 THE COMING OF WAR

The European crisis of 1914 came unexpectedly. The Balkans, likely flashpoint of war, had seen fighting between Bulgaria and Serbia in 1912–13, but the conflicts seemed to have been settled by the intervention of the great European powers. Germany, France and Britain, at least, seemed on friendlier terms than they had been for years.

Assassination at Serajevo

The beginning of the 'colossal war', so long anticipated, was the murder of the Archduke Franz Ferdinand, heir to the throne of the Austrian-Hungarian Empire. On 28 June, he visited Serajevo, capital of Bosnia, to inspect the army. Bosnia, formerly dominated by Turkey, had been annexed by Austria-Hungary in 1908. Its younger inhabitants resented the change: they wanted to belong to Serbia, which they considered to be their national state. With the help of the Serbian 'Black Hand' society, a small group plotted to kill the Archduke. One of them, Gavrilo Princip, shot Franz Ferdinand and his wife as they sat in their open car.

The Archduke Franz-Ferdinand of Austria-Hungary with his wife shortly before they were assassinated in June 1914. Their deaths sparked off the First World War.

A sequence of diplomatic miscalculations followed. When the mobilization of armies began, war was inevitable. The mesh of 'understandings' and actual alliances that grouped the central powers – Germany, Austria and, since 1913, Turkey – against the Triple Entente – France, Russia and Britain – eventually drew most of Europe into the conflict.

On 28 July, Austria-Hungary declared war on Serbia, after a promise of German support. Two days later, Russia, Serbia's ally, fearing the Central Powers' domination of the Balkans and the sea exit from the Black Sea, ordered general mobilization, sending troops to the Austrian and German frontiers. Germany's ultimatum, demanding Russian demobilization, was refused, and she declared war on Russia on 1 August. The German General Staff, fearing a war on two fronts, had a long-standing plan to launch a 'knock-out blow' on France, by a

Restless crowds waiting expectantly outside the Houses of Parliament in London during the war crisis of August 1914.

War fever in London; boys march beside military bands along Whitehall during a recruiting march on 6 August, 1914.

fast-moving advance through Belgium towards Paris. With barely an excuse, Germany declared war on France on 3 August, and her troops began pouring into Luxembourg and then Belgium.

Britain declares war

This invasion brought Britain into the war. The 1839 Treaty of London guaranteed Belgian neutrality: this was the 'scrap of paper' that the Germans now jeered at. On Tuesday, 4 August, Britain sent Germany an ultimatum, demanding withdrawal of her invading armies. When this expired at 11 p.m. (midnight German time), Britain declared war on Germany.

The drama of the last days of peace was heightened by the abrupt arrival of the crisis and the beauty of the 'last summer' of 1914. In late July, the signs of coming war multiplied. On 29 July, the British battle fleet sailed for its war station at Scapa Flow. The City of London was staggered by the closure of the Stock Exchange. The Bank Rate soared from 4 to 10 per cent. Over the August Bank Holiday weekend, panic buying of food began and prices rose sharply. Newspapers – advertised by such placards as 'The brink of catastrophe' or 'Europe drifting to disaster' – were snapped up in the streets. Newly-mobilized soldiers and sailors in uniform mingled with holiday-makers at stations. In London, restless crowds hung about Parliament and Whitehall.

At 11 p.m. on 4 August, the *Times* reporter watched Parliament's clock, Big Ben, signal the arrival of war. 'Was he booming out sweet peace and in red slaughter? At the eleventh stroke of the clock, the crowd burst with one accord into "God save the King". There was no public proclamation that we were at war. ... The great crowd rapidly dispersed in all directions, most of them running to get home quickly,

Men flood to join the Army as volunteers in Southwark, London.

70

This painting depicts the reality of the 1914–18 war. One in every ten Edwardian men under forty-five years of age died in the fighting.

and as they ran they cried aloud rather hysterically, "War! War! War!"'

The war was received with the same sad kind of patriotic enthusiasm in other European capitals. In his sonnet, *Peace*, Rupert Brooke caught the current idea that the declaration was an exciting change after the long dullness of peace:

> Now God be thanked Who has matched us with His hour,
> And caught our youth, and wakened us from sleeping,
> With hand made sure, clear eye and sharpened power,
> To turn, as swimmers into cleanness leaping,
> Glad from a world grown old and cold and weary . . .

As the war settled like a vast grey shadow over Europe, this mood was to be forgotten. Millions died. In Britain, one in every ten Edwardian men under the age of forty-five was killed; one in five wounded. Sorrow and destruction affected almost everybody in the land. The Edwardian era, whose stresses, and political and diplomatic manoeuvring had created the collapse into war, now began to seem, not a 'world grown old and cold and weary' but a lost golden age of peace that ended in the sunlit summer of 1914.

DATE CHART

1901 Death of Victoria. Accession of Edward VII.

Electric trams in London.

Taff Vale case v. Trade Unions.

1902 End of Boer War (began 1899).

Anglo-Japanese alliance. Major Education Act.

1903 First Garden City at Letchworth.

Chamberlain's tariff reform speech.

Daily Mirror began. Women's Social and Political Union (Mrs Pankhurst).

1904 Anglo-French 'entente cordiale'.

First London taxi.

1905 First Moroccan crisis: Anglo-German rivalry heightened.

Motor buses in London.

1906 Liberal government (H. Campbell-Bannermann P.M.).

29 Labour M.P.s.

Reform of British Army began (J. B. Haldane).

First Empire Day (24 May).

Dreadnought battleship launched.

Bakerloo and Piccadilly Underground line opened.

1907 School medical service began.

Anglo-Russian 'entente'.

1908 H. Asquith became Prime Minister.

Old Age Pensions Act.

Olympic games held in London.

First cinema opened.

1909 Bleriot flew the Channel.

Osborne judgement v. Trades Unions.

Selfridges opened.

The 'People's Budget' (D. Lloyd George).

Union of South Africa.

1910 Death of Edward VII. Accession of George V.

Two General Elections (Jan. and Dec.) about

Commons v. Lords dispute.

Post-Impressionist Exhibition in London.

Trans-Atlantic wireless service.

1911 Widespread Trades Union unrest.

Parliament Act limited powers of House of Lords.

National Insurance Act.

Second Moroccan crisis.

1912 Ocean Liner *Titanic* sank.

Irish Home Rule Bill.

National coal strike: more Union unrest.

Balkan wars (to 1913).

1912 Carson's Ulster Covenant.

1913 Triple Alliance of Trades Unions.

Suffragette killed at the Derby.

1914 Violent suffragette campaign.

Curragh mutiny: Ulster crisis.

28 June: assassination of Arch-Duke Franz Ferdinand.

28 July: Austria-Hungary declared war on Serbia.

Chain of declarations of war in Europe.

4 August: Britain declared war on Germany.

GLOSSARY

Aristocracy   The titled nobility.

Constitution   Principles whereby the state is governed.

Derby   An annual horse race run at Epsom in Surrey, England.

Direct action   Pressure for change on a community, using force and not through votes in Parliament.

Dominion   Certain self-ruling territories of the British Empire.

Dreadnought   Fast, powerful, heavily-armoured battleship, with ten twelve-inch guns.

Élite   The top rank of society.

Entente   Friendly understanding between states.

Hierarchy   People placed in rank order.

Home Rule   Self government for Ireland.

Left-wing   Political theory or politician inclining towards Socialism.

Non-conformist   A member of a Protestant sect, outside the Church of England.

Peer   Member of the nobility.

Plutocracy   Very wealthy people not descended from old noble families.

Presbyterian   Member of strict Protestant church originating in Scotland.

Right-wing   Political theory or politician inclining towards Conservatism.

Suffrage   The right to vote in Parliamentary elections.

Suffragettes   Women who agitated to win the vote for their sex.

Syndicalism   French political theory advising Trade Unions to combine into large units and to seize control of key industries, thus giving power to the working class.

Tariff   Customs duty charged on imports or exports.

Veto   Constitutional right of the upper house of the legislature to reject a law proposed by the lower house.

Unionist   Politician favouring the continuing union of Northern Ireland (especially Ulster) with the rest of Britain.

FURTHER READING

General

Cecil, R. *Life in Edwardian England* Batsford, 1969
Degado, A. *Edwardian England* Longman, 1967
Laver, J. *Edwardian Promenade* Hulton, 1958
Read, D. *Edwardian England* Harrap, 1972
Royston Pike, E. *Human Documents of the Lloyd George Era* Allen and Unwin, 1972
Wood, A. *Great Britain 1900–1965* Longman, 1978

Particular aspects

Bentley, N. *Edwardian Album* Cardinal, 1974
Bishop, J. *Social History of Edwardian Britain* Angus and Robertson, 1977
Bourne, G. *Change in the Village* Penguin, 1982
Davidoff, L. *The Best Circles* Croom Helm, 1973
Keating, P. (ed.) *Into Unknown England 1866–1913* Fontana, 1976
London, J. *People of the Abyss* Panther, 1963
Roberts, R. *The Classic Slum* Pelican, 1973
Snellgrove, L. B. *Suffragettes and Votes for Women* Longman, 1984
Winter, G. *A Country Camera* Penguin, 1973

Novels

Forster, E. M. *Howard's End* Penguin, 1910
Sackville-West, V. *The Edwardians* Hogarth, 1930
Wells, H. G. *Kipps* Macmillan, 1905
Wells, H. G. *The War in the Air* Bell, 1908
Wells, H. G. *Tono Bungay* Macmillan, 1909
Wells, H. G. *Ann Veronica* Penguin, 1909
Wells, H. G. *The History of Mr Polly* Nelson, 1910
Williamson, H. *The Dark Lantern* Macdonald, 1951
Williamson, H. *Donkey Boy* Macdonald, 1952
Williamson, H. *Young Philip Maddison* Macdonald, 1953
Williamson, H. *How Dear is Life* Macdonald, 1954

INDEX

PICTURE ACKNOWLEDGEMENTS

BBC Hulton Picture Library 8, 9, 10, 22, 35, 38, 41, 42, 43, 44, 45, 46, 47, 49, 50, 51, 52, 55, 56, 60, 64, 65, 67, 69, 70; Mary Evans Picture Library 11, 13, 15, 20, 21, 23, 28, 30, 31, 32, 34, 37, 40, 48, 53, 57, 61, 62, 63; The Mansell Collection 19, 26, 58; John Topham Picture Library 12, 16, 18, 24, 29, 33, 36, 59, 66, 68; Wayland Picture Library 25, 71